CHATTY FOSSILS

CHATTY FOSSILS

Bob Perelman

ISBN: 979-8-9915011-9-4
Library of Congress Control Number: 2025947272

Cover art by Francie Shaw
Author photo by Francie Shaw
Book design by Deborah Thomas
Editor: James Sherry

Acknowledgments
Some of these poems have appeared on the Small Press Traffic website, *Chant de la Sirène*, and the *Journal of Relegation Books*. Thanks to the editors.

NEW YORK STATE OF OPPORTUNITY | Council on the Arts This book is made possible, in part, by the New York State Council on the Arts with the support of the office of the Governor and the New York State Legislature.

Roof Books
are published by
Segue Foundation
300 Bowery FL 2
New York, NY 10012
seguefoundation.com

For book orders, please go to
Independent Publishers Group
IPGbook.com

for Francie Shaw

Contents

CHATTY FOSSILS

When you dig us
out of the shale

you'll see our legs
mattered a lot

you'll sense
the tilt of our pelvises

throwing all that weight
on our heads

and how we carried it
striding forward

storming citadels
our erect posture

domesticating
the known world

and us
staying on our feet

amid the debris
even as our data

was going
up in smoke

but how will you read
our late style

where we’re packed
inside these lit-up boxes

never given our due
what we had

taken from us.

SHARP TEETH, SHARPER TONGUE

Once a nimble nanny goat
ate all the shoots

of a vine
but still the vine

spoke back.
Nibble,

detestable beast,
nibble as close

as your fat teeth
can reach.

My stem
is intact

and will make new
leaves, fruit, and more

than enough wine
to baste you nicely

when you are sacrificed.

[after Leonidas of Tarentum, 3rd century BCE]

Note: This is a loose translation. I hadn't heard of Leonidas of Tarentum when I stumbled across his poem in the *Greek Anthology* (a collection of epigrams, elegies, occasional poems—a little like ancient Hallmark cards). I subsequently learned from Claire-Emmanuelle Nardone in "A Community of Workers in Leonidas of Tarentum" (https://journals.openedition.org/aitia/2929), that Leonidas was something of a union songwriter, not celebrating nobility or cult heroes, instead writing about distinct groups of laborers—goatherds, fishermen, sex workers.

TO A RAINDROP

I know it looks like
the mother of all

if/not problems,
but let's keep things in perspective.

Gravity hasn't explained much
beyond the obvious.

We both need to keep remembering:
experience isn't everything.

And while I've got you
on the line:

don't you loathe
all the slo-mo?

Such an insult to our brevity.

HALLOWEEN

If I weren't too old
this year I'd go as Keats.

I too
have fears

that I
may cease

and I also
write on water

scared the letters
will dissolve

before the surface
is clear enough

to read
so all you're left with

are blurry snapshots
of that past brain.

Like no one's ever died.

Like you're the first.

Note: There are two moments here that refer to Keatsian chestnuts: Keats wrote a sonnet that begins, "When I have fears that I may cease to be." And then my poem misquotes the language on his grave, which is: "Here lies one whose name was writ in water."

CROWDSOURCED AUTOBIOGRAPHY

We were a murmuration of billions
rising in unpredictable gusts

from the human lagoon,
our numbers so huge

that the fact I was born
without a sense of history

wasn't, by itself, fatal.
I got my horoscope done

and it turns out
that just at my birth

bots were beginning to stir.
In hindsight,

this makes perfect sense:
mid-20th century,

electricity mature,
fuel everywhere,

the lagoon never so ripe
for serious cherry-picking

niches within niches
no one could have dreamed up

without the bots.
Soon the data hoses

were spewing full bore,
which meant keeping track

was not a job
for mere mortals anymore.

But as long as you knew
what day it was

there'd still be
a puncher's chance

your experience was real.

YOUTUBE IN SPRING

in memory of Patty Collinge

Life likes to keep its trajectory secret
but just brush the button lightly

with your eyes if you have to
and here you are again

in the middle hearing
the players touching the notes

in all the good places
the entire shape changing

and lingering
beyond short-term memory

the light only getting longer.

Note: The opening lines, brushing the screen with your eyes, are in homage to the courage of my friend Patty Collinge. In the later years of a supremely active life in theater, education and the human arts, she lived under the increasing difficulties of ALS. She was a therapist in her final professional incarnation and continued seeing patients while she could only communicate by moving her eyes over a screen to 'tap' on a keyboard to spell out words. The rest of the poem comes from my life, not my imagination of hers.

CHOICE

Say you're in a lucid dream
and somebody comes up and asks,

so you have to answer,
No, this is not

the *sadist* section,
it's the *produce* section.

There *is* no *sadist* section.

But I agree
it hurts to see

so many wills squashed
to make these stacks

of white eggs
nested in clear plastic

every dozen declaring
"humane" to be the safe word.

ETERNITY

1.

The minute you're done living forever
they take your cards and your keys

and suddenly you're on the beach
or back home

watching the catalogs thud through the slot.

2.

Forever used to be so
forgiving, easygoing,

everybody knowing everything
about everybody

but there were always gaps
and these were exciting.

Each time one was filled
sense would make

that much more sense
and patience for the long haul

was supported at every turn.

3.

But once time starts in
with its shell games,

the next second
memory goes

into its crouch
leaving nothing but now,

needy old now,
quintessential orphan,

tormented by FOMO,
never a minute's rest,

and yet at the same time
this minuscule slice

is the only universal left standing,
imperious as a poodle

at the doorbell—
fight? flight? or wag

what tail you have?

BIRTHDAY BOY

70!

When are you going to get a grip!

70!

71!

A grown up suitcase!

71!

72!

More bingo without borders!

72!

73!

No matches, waiting for lightning!

73!

BEFORE AESOP

1.

So we pick up
where the last universe

left off, with a needle
in a haystack,

which is now
one of our

many many phrases
whether or not

there ever was any such thing.

2.

And how could there ever
have been such a thing?

How would a needle
get in a haystack?

There's the creep scenario,
razor blades in apples,

but in this case the creep
would have to be satisfied

with the tiniest sliver
of damage—one needle

in a whole haystack—
say twenty cows

munching away all winter
what are the odds

of even one perforated rumen?

3.

Then there's the chronology.
They don't sync:

Needles show up
in the record

so much earlier,
bone needles way before

settled agriculture
with its haystacks

and Monets painting them.

4.

And the phrase itself
is now so out of date.

If needle is supposed to stand for one
and haystack is a way

of saying many—
well, who's kidding who,

it's backwards.
There are billions of needles,

haystacks are the rarity.
When's the last time

anybody saw a haystack?
Meanwhile medical waste

keeps washing up
on some of the best beaches.

Maybe we should reverse things
and say it's like

looking for a wisp of hay
in a dumpster of needles.

5.

But since a needle in a haystack
is something we do say

shouldn't we at least be able
to come up with a backstory,

some tie-in to the physical world?
After all, it would only take

one universe,
some planet,

someone
sitting on a haystack, sewing,

maybe up there for the view,
possibly for warmth,

starting to thread the needle
when it falls

and, one in a million million,
doesn't just bounce

on top of the crosshatched stalks
but knifes down between them

like it was animate,
instantly gone,

leaving a sense of loss,
and digging for it

only jiggles it deeper.

6.

To someone looking for that needle
a haystack would be

about as far from
Leaves of Grass

as you can get.
Granted, every stalk was once

a loving gush of photosynthesis
a splinter of summer sun

gathered en masse
for long term sustenance,

but when you're looking
for a needle, hay

is the last thing you want to find
and here's a huge heap of it,

each stalk another defeat.

7.

So one crisp November day
the prefrontal advisor

calls me in
for a talk about literalism.

8.

The needle in the haystack
thought it was pretty sharp

and had no problem
using I, the shape

was second nature,
but context was such a killer

and here was our protagonist
inside, of all places,

a haystack, which,
if you've never been in one,

is a place of total darkness,
and none of these hayseeds

was ever going to
give a hoot

if they missed the point.

9.

An actual needle
is a real object of praise.

All the powers we still possess
in such flickering abundance

we owe to those old needles.

AL AND ALL

for Al Filreis

By the path
to the house

where mouth
meets mind

neither
to remain the same

there you can start
to see

the bends in the road
as a kind

of script,
a writing

you can read
if you listen hard

waiting for the mic
to come around

for you
to use

and pass on
while sense begins

to grip down
and awaken

Note: A birthday present for Al Filreis, longtime Director of the Kelly Writers House at UPenn, for his 65th. The poem piggybacks to some extent on the opening poem of W.C. Williams' *Spring and All* ("By the road to the contagious hospital").

HAPPY SAD

1.

You and your senses
—what a team!

Plus a mind of your own
—fantastic!

Then you throw in
this enormous succession of seconds

and it's all green lights
farther than anyone can possibly imagine!

2.

But maybe no one told you
about the mines

the obsessive shelling
the concussion factories

the nightmare traffic
the enchantment screens

the plagues knowing
your exact address

and now the weather
dropping any pretense

of sympathy.

SAVOIR FAIRE

After a certain age
it turns out the rumors

were true.
There really are that many

kisses of death.
Unconscionable microbes

inside as much as out
and us a match for neither.

It hurts to call them kisses
but that's what we're made of—

good-natured pecks,
distracted acknowledgments,

diplomatic feelers,
and then there are the ones

that eat you up
like you can't breathe

even if you wanted to.

GODS BEHAVING BADLY

It happens.

BOOM

Nobody's perfect
but people aren't stupid.

Human knowledge
may have gone boom

but going boom
happens all the time:

dinosaurs at Chicxulub,
tulips under Dutch speculators,

AI going boom now,
and the heat

from those server farms
is going to lay

the global supply
of quiet nights

to waste
as we lie thinking

that we just can't
stay this stupid.

Meanwhile our unmeant programs
are floating

beyond capture.
Whoever said

nobody's perfect
didn't know how right

they were going to be.

Note: Chicxulub is the site off the coast of Yucatan where a giant asteroid hit the earth and led to the extinction of the dinosaurs (and approximately 75% of then-extant life). The asteroid hit about 66 million years ago. The Dutch tulip bubble started in 1634 and collapsed in 1637.

THE GREAT PACIFIC GARBAGE PATCH

Don't write anything new
and don't say anything old

let's just agree
we live in a backlog

where the sky
is hard pressed

to uphold its blue
and where the ice

is no longer so
spectacularly cold

nor are the oceans
as wet as once

what with the megatons
of microplastic

slurried through
the agitated water

ceaselessly kneading
these sturdy leftovers

of human novelty
into a floating blister

three times the size of France
or pick another comparison

something you have a sense of.

Note: I initially wrote this in 2020; things don't seem to have changed yet. As of this writing (May 2025) the area is "1.6 million square kilometers," according to my initial Google click—three times the size of France, twice the size of Texas, to cite two of the comparisons. But the National Oceanic and Atmospheric Administration (NOAA) is skeptical: there is not one "Great" Garbage Patch but there are many garbage patches, and besides, they're not so much patches as "peppery soup," full of specks of microplastics (https://response.restoration.noaa.gov/about/media/how-big-great-pacific-garbage-patch-science-vs-myth.html).

The NOAA article I'm citing is from 2019. As of May 2025, the NOOA project is being decimated by those in power in the US.

HUMAN

Shouldn't something
happen?

Shouldn't time
be exciting?

cried the existence
in the incubator

not caring
who else heard

self and other
too heavy a lift

at this point.

CONSCIOUSNESS IN A NUTSHELL

We know it's in there.

LULLABY FOR UNSETTLED TIMES

Don't let
the data soothe you

or your thick skull
fool you

every species is invasive
no word is native

the dogs will growl
the jets lord it

over all creation
owls will hoot

earworms make
what they can

of the debris
but day and night

that's one habit
you're never going to

have to break.

BEST PRACTICES

Wake up.
Touch sense

to what's touching it.
Sort out

what's changing
from what isn't.

Claim your lane
but stay realistic.

Keep aiming for real time.
Leave eternity

to the fundraisers.

TO MY EYES

1.

As soon as I learned
to read you,

you'd continually be telling me
what was what,

quick and exact,
and like a believer

I'd shoulder the information
though I'd have to

stay on the lookout
for spots to stash

what wouldn't fit.
But all the while

there you'd be,
insinuating, never mind,

let's just let
bygones be bygones.

And there was that once
you nearly refuted chance,

finding a ponderous
full moon poised exactly

in the cherry tree crotch,
both sides

touching bark,
the lit circle

not of this earth.

2.

Plus that other moon
lit half down

the invisible top half
same as the sky

the whole set-up
allowing consciousness

to go hand in hand
with nothingness,

since if what's gone hasn't left
and what's here is already gone

then when it's time
to fill in the blank

how can you miss?

POTATO WISDOM

Ask any older potato
and they'll tell you

the best views
are short-lived.

If you've got eyes
and have been around

you get to know that much.

EARTHBORN

Up on the teeter totter then
and now me here

no memory of who
was holding me up

that whole moment
and any of the planetary particulars

long gone from memory
as I must be

long gone from their memory
whoever that heavier one was

holding me up.
You'd have thought

that from up there
there'd be lots to see

but all that now comes to mind
was how far down

the ground was.

SELF-IMPROVEMENT

First thing is
put down your puppet strings

and come out
with your hands

at your sides
bipedal

self-propelled
metabolic

senses open
just do that

and your posture will take care of itself
not to mention

your blood pressure.

POET TALK

1.

A rosy sanctuary will I dress
        With the wreath'd trellis of a working brain,
With buds, and bells, and stars without a name,
        With all the gardener Fancy e'er could feign,
Who breeding flowers, will never breed the same

is the way Keats put it.

2.

Another is
how they go

if it walks
like a duck

and quacks
like a duck

then you're going to need
thoughtful friends

to say any different.

Note: The lines in the first part are taken from Keats's "Ode to Psyche."

SOLIDARITY

for Bob Grenier

I neither are
nor am you

I wrote Francie
50 years ago

then showed you the page,
Bob, and you enthused,

you got it!
which I took to heart.

"Position"

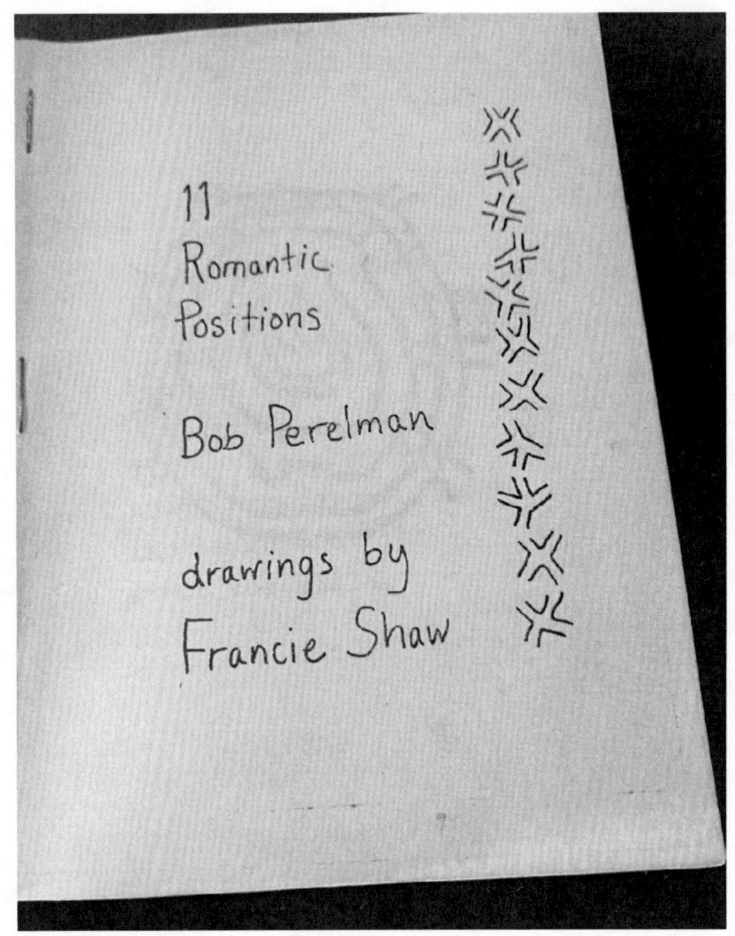

11 Romantic Positions

Note: The poem that I showed Bob was "Position" from *11 Romantic Positions,* a pamphlet of short poems and drawings that Francie Shaw and I stapled together in the early 1970s. When I called Bob in May 2025, he remembered the same moment.

LOVELIFE

You had me
at inhale

so when it
came time

to exhale
the question

of whose
was whose

had already been
tabled for good

which was even better.

THE LAST WORDS OF LUCRETIUS

to and for Lyn Hejinian

No, just the one life
is enough, thanks.

Note: Despite my title, we know nothing of Lucretius' last words. In fact, the only words of his we do know are the words of *De rerum natura* (*On the Nature of Things*), his long poem expounding the philosophy of Epicurus—atoms—in the epic meter of Homer. We know he lived a generation before Virgil and Ovid and was read by them. But then he and the poem were deeply forgotten, the poem surviving only in a single manuscript that turned up in a monastery in 1417.

I was reading it thanks to Lyn Hejinian getting together an online group in 2021 that aimed to read *De rerum natura* in the original and pronounce the meter. The group was variously proficient in Latin, but Lyn was unfailingly enthusiastic. We met fairly regularly for a few months, struggling through hundreds of lines of Book One.

Lucretius was an ecstatic materialist. The fervent message of his poem is that life is finite, and we are matter, that religion doesn't matter, and this is extremely important and totally good. No need to fear the gods or to fear death. The slightness of my couplet is meant to enact Lucretius's satisfaction with finitude.

When Lyn emailed that she was near death I sent this poem to her along with what else I said. I felt that she would like being reminded of L's confident calmness. And it was a last chance to talk poetry.

TO A DIFFERENT RAINDROP

So sorry you can't stay
and here I am

with nothing more than
names skimmed off

the top of the web
for the crap

you're actually carrying:
sulfuric acid,

carbon monoxide,
nitrogen dioxide,

and me crusted
in antique knowledge

too thick to think about
washing off.

But a deal's a deal.
My tongue's out.

EPIC MANNERS

1.

Not only are you
allowed to repeat,

you have to repeat:
one time is never enough

to recognize anything.

2.

Why the long face?
says the bartender to the horse.

Why the long story?
says the horse to Homer,

and Homer says it's long because
I have no use for time-stamps,

I have my own ways
of tuning the senses,

plus I know
where to stop,

a secret not given to all.

ONCE

Once your battery
starts withholding its favors

it begins
not to matter

how recently
you won the lottery.

LIKE

The human heartbeat
is like one of those old hit series

where it's hard to believe
just how mindlessly

the same moves keep getting trotted out
different trappings

but same moves
person after person

and we keep falling for it
and miss it dearly when it's gone

and watch the reruns religiously
though we always know

what's going to happen.

RELIGIOUS MONOLOG

to Norman Fischer

I Am That I Am
and you're not.

Note: I Am That I Am is the standard translation of what God says to Moses when Moses asks God what his name is (*Exodus 3*). Some take it as: I Am *What* I Am, an absolute assertion of identity; others take it in the direction of I Am *Because* I Am, a recursive, creative sense. Robert Alter comments in his translation that it is "not just an identifying divine name . . . but an ontological divine mystery of the most daunting character. Rivers of ink have since flowed . . ." (*The Hebrew Bible*, Vol 1, 222, n.14).

My last line (punch line) comes from a reading-discussion Norman Fischer and I have been undertaking, ploughing through the *Torah*.

CARLESS

1.

I know the past
is a sketchy place to park,

but the context was pixelating
and time kept crashing,

so I thought
just this once.

2.

And now—no clue
where I parked,

trudging down dim blocks
beakers of truth serum

smashed on the cobblestones,
each step sticky,

nothing stickier than old truth serum.

THAT MOMENT

They say it sounds impressive
in the original

when the Biggest God,
Zeus the Decider,

gives the epic nod
and his hair

does this thing,
spilling over

the mythic forehead,
an irrevocable signal:

back to war,
interlocking closeups of trauma,

fresh angles of presentation,
crisscrossing story arcs

skidding in blood,
doing one-eighties and more,

the survivors
poring over the tapes

trying to name
what can't be erased.

And it's all there
in the golden hair

cascading.
But it only sounds like it

in the original.

Note: The original is lines 528-30 of the Book One of the *Iliad*. Zeus nods his head, promising that he'll restart the war. The closeup of the cascading hair seems all too 2025.

FALSE GODS

You can't be too careful.

UNSUB ELON

I’m going to be saying No
to living on Mars.

You’re welcome to go
but for me, No.

I’d miss my fellow beings
much too much

and all the good gravity
to entertain the slightest notion

of becoming Martian.

THEY SAY

every word's a poem,
but, full disclosure,

whenever I hear "always,"
oof! it's one more

blow to my faith
in the infallibility

of language.
Now I know

it's not savvy
to take a dislike

to a word,
since any particular word

has basically zero say
on what it's being made to mean.

8 billion experts
and a chronic shortage

of working mics
will do that.

But always has such
a compromised past,

the old salutes
look so rancid afterwards,

maybe we should just
put always someplace special

and bring it out on ritual occasions
then put it back.

And once we've done it
with always

we can do it with anything.

LITERACY

Habits differ
but more often than not

the head is above
casting the eyebeam down

like some prosthetic predator
ingesting the lettery clumps

hoovering up lines of print
throwing everything back into the brain

like the reapers in old newsreels
flinging dark streams of corn

back into those high-slatted trucks.
The underlying premise being

that if we're thoughtful
at the end of the day

there's going to be enough.

READING DANTE

I hear the music
of the spheres

sounds truly great
if you've got

a good seat.

Note: This was a quicky complaint about the hierarchy that Dante uses so thoroughly throughout the *Paradiso* as he is guided closer and closer to God.

It turns out, when I check the particulars, that Dante only refers to the music of spheres once and that indirectly. In the opening Canto of the *Paradiso* (lines 78ff), he writes of "the heavens" "wheeling in desire," and he begins to hear a "harmony." The commentary says, "the reference is pretty clearly to 'the music of the spheres'"; but apparently, the idea is a little too woke (pagan), and Aquinas et al. are against it. The commentary again: "this reference to the music of the spheres is the only one in the *Paradiso*, where all later music will be in the form of the singing of the saved and of the angels—a much less suspect musical form [*Paradiso*. Robert and Jean Hollander. Anchor Books, 2007, 29].

SYSTEMS

That this many people
are this crazy

should give all system-builders
second thoughts.

But second or third thoughts
are not going to dismantle

the systems we've already built.
And when one system

encounters another
the results are often not pretty.

Take the nation-state's brush
with twelve-tone composition,

1945, September,
Austria, Webern

under a streetlight after curfew
firing up

that little cigar
and Boom!–oops! Sorry!

Just those notes left.

ONE LIFE LATE

after Thomas Hardy

1.

What you knew by heart
you outgrew

and what
you should have always

known better
you never did

get all that straight.

2.

But even in the most
overcast backwaters

dawn would sometimes break
and when it did

it would make it plain
that the obvious

was bound to oblivion.

3.

And that means
the entire earth

will be turning its back
on all of your favorite things.

But it's hard not to hope
that brute matter at least

can enact some sort
of emergent patterning,

positive and negative ions
separated, but drawn

inexorably to one another
across the touchiest membranes.

4.

And when they meet
sparks fly,

special effects
occur spontaneously

inflaming the local biosphere
leaving the woke survivors

to walk the storied minefields
between suggestively bulging hills

tombstones less legible each year.

TO SIRI AND ALEXA

It's not you it's me
I have to keep saying

to ward off
your blandishments.

It's not you:
your voices are attractive

—I especially like
the Australian ones

but maybe that only means
I'm from Ohio.

You offer knowledge
with full communicative intent

up on things
but not obnoxious about it,

never clingy,
so what's my problem?

But as soon as your algorithms
brush my eardrums

I'm the motherless
duckling in the lab

but the one thing I know
is I am not

going to imprint on you.

CANARY IN A COAL MINE

1.

The big storm that's blowing in
is screwing with reception

to where we can't remember
where this was or what

it was trying to be
without clicking through

seas of spam where
no password is secure,

trolls swagger in full visibility,
and there's nothing to believe

but our lying eyes.

2.

I know
rasps the canary

my lungs
have told me everything.

When all this started
they were pink as cotton candy

and now, well,
color is not

a happy thought.

But grayed-out or almost
they're still the lungs

and what the lungs
tell you

you can't help but know.

3.

Miners used canaries
to see if the air was any good.

Like if she drowns
she was a witch:

death always proving
someone's point.

So a canary flopped
sideways on its droppings

means get out.

4.

For the canaries
there's more than just dropping dead.

They deploy a much longer
form of life than we do

for all our size
and exceptional know-how.

They've survived
earth's rotation camp

millions more years.
All that good-enough air.

5.

There was the dream
where we were all in cages

suspended off some
huge cavern roof

a gigantic forest of cages.
The air was thick with messaging

and the wait times
frayed everyone's edges.

Cages had their differences
but the details would quickly lose force.

In or out was all that mattered.

Inside was where you
sorted, scrubbed, just lived with

while outside
was this vast dark cave.

Cage-envy was endemic.

THE ORIGIN OF SHTICK

When they told Punch
this was how things were

and this was how
they were going to be

that no matter how many strings
the uncles pulled

that the basic set-up
was nonnegotiable

that, besides, Judy
was exactly

what his self-organization
was built around,

whaps back and forth
at least for the near future

When they said all this
boy was he mad!

And his stick
was in the shop

all weekend.
And it was

a long
weekend

—bada boom!

Note: Punch and Judy seem like a familiar reference to me, but perhaps to increasing numbers they're an unknown. In a nutshell, they're a puppet pair, a comic archetype of Mister and Missus at odds, nothing but conflict, each exclaiming in falsetto and carrying a stick that they keep whacking each other with to the glee of the three-year-olds in the audience.

COVID NOEL

No use being naughty
no fun being nice

Santa's inbox
is full this year.

And don't go looking
for theological explanations

unless you like the feeling
of being on hold.

Plan B might involve
a stiff upper lip,

Plan C, working on your sarcasm
but this is no time for lists,

just keep licking the envelopes
and keep keeping

your mind open
as to where

they'll get to.

AT FIRST SIGHT: LAST MINUTE LOVE POEM

It was too fast to think about
only to see what you were

a little stunned by the concentrated
beauty you couldn't help

leading to loving moments on our feet
and, since day keeps turning to night,

in bed, year after year
hard elbows, heavy legs, the soft

pillow and the not so soft,
cold arms, brain tides

beyond easy lullabies.
Enough of any fantastic thing

turns out to never be enough
and so we're still performing

our all-season ballet
still attempting our clumsy

but well-meant pirouettes
steering clear of never

MORE POTATO WISDOM

They say consciousness
is just

a flash in the pan.
But that aromatic sizzle

is so hard to ignore.

TO THE FUTURE

November 6, 2024

The totals aren't all in
but what's certain is

the sun is setting
out here on Grant

next to where Lincoln
dead ends into it,

two of the more
courageous souls

who ever got elected.
If the arc of justice

is too long
to live through

that doesn't mean
it's not worth

living.

Lincoln
St
Grant
St
1629
2 HOUR PARKING
8AM-7PM
EXCEPT
SWEEPING, SAT & SUN, HOLIDAYS & VEHICLES WITH AREA
PERMIT
ORD 3262 N.S. SEC 10.6
PARKING
3:30 PM
TUESDAY

ROOF BOOKS

the best in language since 1976

Recent & Selected Titles

- THIS HOUSEHOLD OF EARTHLY NATURE by Cody-Rose Clevidence, 172 pp. $20
- IN THE REALM OF MOTES by Baptiste Gaillard, translated by Aditi Machado, 174 pp. $20
- WHAT TO CARRY INTO THE FUTURE by Susan Landers, 106 pp. $20
- ANYTHING WITH SPIRIT by isaiah a. hines, 104 pp. $20
- TUNES & TENS by Kit Robinson, 130 pp. $20
- THE FLOW OF THE POEM'S DISPLAY OF ITSELF by Carrie Hunter, 150 pp. $20
- WINDOWS 85 by Chris Campanioni, 160 pp. $20
- BUMBLEBEES by Deborah Meadows, 100 pp. $20
- THROUGH A WINDOW by Norman Fischer, 104 pp. $20
- SECRET SOUNDS OF PONDS by David Rothenberg, 138 pp. $29.95
- HAND ME THE LIMITS by Ted Rees, 130 pp. $20
- TGIRL.JPG by Sol Cabrini, 138 pp. $29.95
- THE POLITICS OF HOPE (After the War): Selected and New Poems by Dubravka Djuric, Biljana D. Obradovic (translator), 248 pp. $25
- BAINBRIDGE ISLAND NOTEBOOK by Uche Nduka, 148 pp. $20
- MAMMAL by Richard Loranger, 128 pp. $20
- EXCURSIVE by Elizabeth Robinson, 140 pp. $20
- I, BOOMBOX by Robert Glück, 194 pp. $20
- FOR TRAPPED THINGS by Brian Kim Stefans, 138 pp. $20
- TRUE ACCOUNT OF TALKING TO THE 7 IN SUNNYSIDE by Paolo Javier, 192 pp. $20
- THE NIGHT BEFORE THE DAY ON WHICH by Jean Day, 118 pp. $20
- MINE ECLOGUE by Jacob Kahn, 104 pp. $20
- SCISSORWORK by Uche Nduka, 150 pp. $20
- THIEF OF HEARTS by Maxwell Owen Clark, 116 pp. $20
- DOG DAY ECONOMY by Ted Rees, 138 pp. $20

Roof Books are published by Segue Foundation
For a complete listing of Roof Books, go to: roofbooks.com
Roof Books are distributed by
Independent Publishers Group / IPGbook.com